SINGAPORE
TRAVEL GUIDE
2023

Charles B. Hogan

SINGAPORE TRAVEL GUIDE 2023

A Singapore Travel Guide for First Timers: Uncovering the Best Hidden Gems, Exploring Singapore's Unique Tourist Attractions, and Planning the Perfect Tour

BY

Charles B. Hogan

ALL RIGHTS RESERVED.

No part of this publication may be reproduced, distributed or transmitted in any form or by any means including photocopying, recording or other electronic or mechanical methods without the prior written permission of the publisher, except in the case of brief quotations embedded in critical reviews and certain other noncommercial uses permitted by copyright law.

Copyright © Charles B. Hogan, 2023

Table of Contents

My Singapore Travel Experience

Introduction

Brief History of Singapore

Culture

Ethnic groups

Religion

Geography

Population

Climate

Chapter 1. Basic Travel Tips

1. When to Visit Singapore

2. How to get to Singapore

3. Best Time to Visit Singapore

4. Things to do when you get to Singapore

5. Best Places to Stay in Singapore

Chapter 2: Travel Preparation

6. Entry Requirements

7. Types of Travelers Visa

8. Singapore Visa on Arrival

9. Singapore Travel Restrictions

Chapter 3: Transport and Accommodations

10. Getting Around

11. Accommodations in Singapore

   Hotels:

   Hostels:

   Guesthouses:

   Resort:

   Service Apartment

   Vacation rentals

Chapter 4: Learn About The Currency

12. Singapore currency

13. Where to Exchange Money in Singapore

14. Tipping

15. Money and Budgeting

16. Language

17. General travel advice

Chapter 5: Attraction and sightseeing

18. National Parks

19. Beaches

20. Islands

21. Temples

22. Museums

Chapter 6: Activities in Singapore

23. Outdoor Adventures

24. Food and Drink

  Traditional Dishes:

  Local Street Foods :

  Drinks:

25. Singapore Étiquettes.

26. Shopping in Singapore

27. Souvenirs:

28. Handicrafts in Singapore

Chapter 7: Cultural Experience

29. Festival

30. Music and dance

Chapter 8: The Best 7 days Singapore Itinerary

31. Best 7 days Itinerary

Day 1: Merlion statue

Day 2: Colonial District

Day 3: Jurong Bird park

Day 4: Science Centre

Day 5: National Museum

Day 6: Singapore Flyer

Day 7: Botanic Garden

Chapter 9: Safety And Security

32. Rules and Regulations
33. Singapore Safety
34. Singapore Emergency Numbers

Chapter 10: Conclusion

My Singapore Travel Experience

My recent trip to Singapore was one of the most memorable experiences of my life. I got the chance to tour this magnificent city with my family and friends.

To start with, I was amazed by the breathtaking skyline of Singapore. From the Marina Bay Sands hotel to the Singapore Flyer, the vista was just stunning. I also got the opportunity to see the famed Merlion monument and the stunning Gardens by the Sea.

The following day, we did a city tour and saw some of the most prominent tourist sites in Singapore. We visited the famed Singapore Zoo, Jurong Bird Park, and the Singapore Botanic

Gardens. We also got the opportunity to experience the local cuisine and try some typical Singaporean delicacies.

On the third day, we took a day excursion to Sentosa Island. We visited the Universal Studios theme park, the S.E.A. Aquarium, and the Adventure Cove Waterpark. It was a terrific day packed with loads of fun and adventure.

The final day of our vacation was spent shopping. We visited some of the major shopping malls in Singapore and explored the bustling street markets. We also experienced some of the local dishes, such as the famed Singapore chicken rice.

Overall, my vacation to Singapore was a fantastic experience. I got the chance to tour the city, enjoy the culture, and sample some delicious cuisine. I would recommend a trip to Singapore to anyone who wants to have an amazing experience.

Introduction

Singapore is a tiny island republic situated off the southern point of the Malay Peninsula in Southeast Asia. It is a dynamic, busy city-state that is recognized for its variety, modernity, and historical and cultural attractions. With a population of little over 5.6 million people, Singapore is one of the most densely inhabited nations in the world.

Blessed with a tropical environment and over 200 ethnicities, Singapore is a melting pot of many cultures and ideas. This has produced a unique combination of cuisines, cultures, and lifestyles that makes Singapore a wonderful location to visit.

From its early days as a British trading post to its modern-day stature as a global financial and business hub, Singapore has a fascinating history. It has been a leader in urban planning, public housing, and public transportation, and is home to some of the world's most iconic landmarks, such as the Marina Bay Sands and the iconic Merlion statue.

Singapore is a major tourist destination, with a range of attractions for visitors to explore. From its bustling shopping streets and nightlife to its numerous museums and galleries, there is something for everyone. Singapore also has some of the world's best beaches, parks, and gardens, and is an ideal destination for outdoor activities.

Singapore is also home to a wealth of cultural and religious sites, from Hindu temples to Buddhist and Taoist shrines. There is also a booming art, music, and film industry, as well as a busy nightlife and night markets.

Singapore is a popular location for visitors, business travelers, and ex-pats alike. With its world-class infrastructure, an abundance of attractions, and multicultural vibrancy, Singapore is a truly unique destination that is sure to delight and enchant.

Brief History of Singapore

Singapore has a lengthy and rich history that extends back centuries before it was proclaimed an independent republic in 1965. The island has been inhabited for at least 2,000 years, and archaeological evidence shows that it was a lively commercial port in the 14th century.

In the 16th century, Singapore was conquered by the Portuguese, who dubbed it "Singapura". It was soon taken over by the Dutch, who promptly changed its name to "Batavia". The Brits finally took possession of the island in 1819 and it became a significant commercial center for the British East India Company.

During World War II, Singapore was captured by the Japanese and suffered massive casualties. Following the war, Singapore was given self-governance in 1959 and formally named an independent republic in 1965.

Singapore has since evolved into one of the most successful and richest nations in the world, due to its ideal location, highly educated people, and strong government regulations. It is currently a bustling city with a robust economy and a good level of life.

Despite its fast expansion, Singapore remains a culturally and historically rich location. Tourists may visit its various museums and galleries, which showcase relics from its lengthy history, as well as its colorful street markets, eclectic architecture, and beautiful gardens. There is also a strong arts and entertainment scene, with a broad range of taverns, clubs, and restaurants.

Singapore is a country that has gone a long way from its modest origins, and its lengthy and rich history is a monument to its endurance and drive.

Culture

Singapore is a multi-ethnic nation with a rich cultural background. Chinese, Malay, Indian, and several other ethnic groups have all joined together to produce the unique culture that is Singapore today.

The Chinese are the biggest ethnic group in Singapore and represent the majority of the population. Chinese culture is greatly affected by Confucianism and Buddhism, and ancient rituals like ancestor worship and the Chinese New Year are still practiced. Chinese Singaporeans are also renowned for their love of cuisine, and classic dishes like Hainanese Chicken Rice and Bak Kut

Teh are popular among residents and visitors alike.

Malays make up the second biggest ethnic group in Singapore, and their culture has been profoundly affected by Islam. Malay culture is distinguished by its strong feeling of community and hospitality, and Malay traditions such as the Malay wedding ceremony and the Hari Raya Aidilfitri celebration are major components of Singapore's cultural environment.

The Indian population in Singapore is made up of predominantly Tamil and Sikh immigrants, and their culture is highly influenced by the Hindu faith, with the Diwali festival and the Thaipusam parade being the most significant festivals. Indian food is also popular in Singapore, with dishes such as Briyani, Roti

Prata, and Tandoori Chicken being commonly accessible.

In addition to the primary ethnic groups, Singapore is home to a sizable expatriate population from all over the globe. This has further expanded the culture of the country, and foreign events such as the Great Singapore Sale, Christmas, and Halloween are celebrated with flair.

Singapore is also famed for its contemporary and efficient infrastructure, with the world-class Changi Airport and the landmark Marina Bay Sands hotel being just two examples of the country's great accomplishments.

In conclusion, Singapore is a lively and diversified country that is home to a broad variety of cultures and customs. From the ancient Chinese, Malay, and Indian holidays to current multinational events, Singapore culture is genuinely distinct and something to be treasured.

Ethnic groups

Singapore is a thriving and diversified nation, with a population of around 5.6 million people. The population of Singapore is made up of three primary ethnic groups: Chinese, Malays, and Indians. Each of these groups has its own culture and traditions, making the people of Singapore a melting pot of varied origins.

The Chinese are the majority ethnic group in Singapore, making up about 74.3% of the population. Chinese culture is highly significant to the people of Singapore and they celebrate several traditional festivals that are recognized in the Chinese calendar.

The Malays are the second biggest ethnic group, making up around 13.4% of the population. The Malays are mostly Muslims and are passionately committed to their Islamic religion. They have their distinct language and culture, which can be observed in many districts of Singapore.

The Indians are the third biggest ethnic community in Singapore, making up around 9.2% of the population. They are predominantly Hindus and are passionately attached to their religion. They have their distinct language and culture, which can be observed in many districts of Singapore.

Visitors visiting Singapore will encounter a dynamic and diversified culture that is full of life and energy. People in Singapore are kind and always prepared to assist. Singaporeans are also quite proud of their nation and are always ready to show tourists around.

No matter what your origin or culture, you will be welcomed with open arms in Singapore. It is a terrific destination to come and explore, and the people of Singapore will make your stay a memorable one.

Religion

Singapore is generally regarded as a religiously diverse and tolerant culture. Religion plays a vital part in the lives of many Singaporeans, with around 43.2% of the population identifying as

Buddhist, 18.3% as Taoism, 14.3% as Muslim, 11.3% as Hindu, and 7.0% as Christian. Other faiths, including Judaism and Sikhism, account for the remaining 6.0%.

The Singapore government views the practice of religion as an important factor in maintaining social harmony and cohesion. As such, the Singapore Government has taken several steps to ensure that religious harmony is maintained and that religion remains an important part of Singaporean life.

Buddhism is the most frequently practiced religion in Singapore, and it has been present in the nation since the 19th century. Buddhism is founded on the teachings of Siddhartha Gautama, a spiritual teacher from India who reached enlightenment in the 6th century BCE.

Buddhism is a non-theistic religion, meaning it does not entail any belief in a deity or gods. Buddhists in Singapore practice their religion via meditation, the observation of moral commandments, and charitable activities.

Taoism is another important religion in Singapore, and it was brought to the area in the late 19th century. Taoism is founded on the teachings of Laozi, a Chinese philosopher who flourished in the 6th century BCE. Taoism is a philosophical and religious tradition that stresses balance, harmony, and simplicity. Taoists in Singapore practice their beliefs via meditation and the observation of religious ceremonies, such as ancestor worship.

Islam is the second-largest religious group in Singapore and has also been present in the nation since the 19th century. Islam is a monotheistic faith founded on the teachings of the prophet Muhammad, and it is the official religion of the nation of Singapore. Muslims in Singapore practice their faith through the observance of Islamic laws and rituals, as well as through charity and social justice.

Christianity is the third-largest religious group in Singapore and has been present in the country since the 19th century. Christianity is a monotheistic religion founded on the teachings of Jesus, who is regarded by Christians to be the son of God. Christians in Singapore exercise their religion via church attendance, the observance of Christian ceremonies, and charitable deeds.

Hinduism is a minority religion in Singapore, and it was initially brought to the area in the late 19th century. Hinduism is a polytheistic religion founded on the teachings of the Vedas, a collection of ancient books written in Sanskrit. Hindus in Singapore exercise their religion via the observation of religious ceremonies, such as puja, and charity deeds.

In addition to the five main faiths, Singapore also boasts a sizable non-religious community. This category comprises persons who identify as an atheist, agnostics, or secular humanists. The non-religious population in Singapore is expanding, and it is believed that 20% of the population is non-religious.

In Singapore, there is a great focus on religious tolerance and mutual respect. Individuals of diverse origins and faiths are encouraged to live in peace with one another, and the government has several efforts in place to foster religious understanding and harmony.

Geography

Situated on the southern point of Southeast Asia, roughly 100 kilometers north of the equator, Singapore is a New-York-City- size island and city-nation on the western side of the South China Sea. Listed as the 192nd biggest nation in the world, it occupies 725 square kilometers (approximately 280 square miles) and is 40 kilometers long and 20 kilometers broad at its widest point. It's becoming larger all the time as more and more land is recovered from the sea. At about 7,800 inhabitants per square kilometer, it is the third most densely inhabited territory or country in the world after Macau and Hong Kong. Singapore is nearly 3.5 times the size of Washington D.C.

Singapore is positioned in Southeast Asia between Malaysia and Indonesia at the narrowest point of the Strait of Malacca, one of the world's major marine lanes linking the Indian Ocean with the South China Sea. Situated off the southern point of the Malay Peninsula, Singapore is linked to Malaysia by a causeway, which traverses the mile-wide Straits of Johor between Singapore and Malaysia. Singapore is also just a few kilometers away from the Indonesian island of Sumatra. Between Singapore and Sumatra sits the eastern end of the 890-kilometer-long Straits of Malacca, one of the world's busiest maritime waterways. It is no wonder that Singapore has been named the world's busiest port.

An island republic with no land borders, Singapore includes one main island and 58 islands. The overall shoreline in 2005 was 193 kilometers. The land area stated by the government in 2004 was 699 square kilometers; the water area was 10 square kilometers, for a total national area of 709 square kilometers.

Between 1988 and 2005, the shoreline extended by 55 kilometers and the overall land area rose by roughly 63 square kilometers as a consequence of substantial land reclamation and landfill operations. Singapore claims a territorial sea area of three nautical miles, as well as an exclusive fishing zone outside the territorial sea as specified in treaties and practice.

Population

Singapore's overall population was at 5.64 million at the end-June 2022. The overall population expanded by 3.4 percent from the previous year, mostly owing to the rise in the non-resident population. Although the overall population recovered after two consecutive years of decrease, it remained slightly below the pre-COVID level of 5.70 million as of end-June 2019.

The resident population expanded by 2.2 percent from 2021 to 4.07 million as of end-June 2022. Within the resident population, citizens grew by 1.6 percent to 3.55 million while permanent residents grew by 6.3 percent to 0.52 million.

The growth in the resident population could be largely attributed to the easing of travel restrictions due to COVID-19, as more citizens and PRs who were previously overseas continuously for 12 months or more returned to Singapore. The non-resident population grew by 6.6 percent to 1.56 million over the same period but was still lower than the pre-COVID level of 1.68 million as of end-June 2019.

Climate

Singapore is in the equatorial monsoon region of Southeast Asia, and its climate is characterized by uniformly high temperatures and nearly constant precipitation throughout the year. The average monthly temperature varies from about 81° F (27° C) in June to 77° F (25° C) in

January. The daily range is somewhat greater, averaging about 13° F (7° C).

Singapore's maritime location and constant humidity, however, keep maximum temperatures relatively moderate: the highest temperature ever recorded was only 97° F (36° C).

The seasons are defined by the relative incidence of rainfall, which, in turn, is determined by the movements of the monsoon air masses. The wettest and windiest time occurs during the northeast monsoon (November–March), with rainfall reaching an average monthly high of more than 10 inches (250 mm) in December. Conversely, the season with the least amount of rainfall and the lightest winds occurs during the southwest monsoon (May–September), with rainfall plummeting to a monthly low of fewer than 7 inches in July.

April through October are inter-monsoonal times marked by slow air patterns and strong afternoon showers and thunderstorms. Overall, Singapore's precipitation averages roughly 95 inches annually, and rain falls somewhere on the island every day of the year.

Chapter 1. Basic Travel Tips

1. When to Visit Singapore

1. December to early March

Consistent rainfall is recorded during this season, especially from December to early January.

Temperature: Avg. of 30° high to 24° low

Weather: December is the wettest month in Singapore with rainfall ranging from 63mm to 766mm. So, if you are planning your visit during this period, you need not worry. You may still discover the finest spots to visit in Singapore without any worry.

Significance: Important events and festivals during these months include Christmas, ZoukOut Music festival, Pongal, Marina Bay Singapore New Year's countdown, Chinese New Year, Singapore Carnival, Fringe Festival, etc.

Why you should visit now: The mood is quite festive and joyous at this time because of Christmas, New Year, and Chinese New Year happening in December and January. One may explore and observe the vivacious side of Singapore at this time. Singapore provides the most exciting Christmas events, carnivals, New Year's celebrations, and fireworks.

Know before you visit: Monsoons occur from December to March in Singapore, with December receiving the most rainfall. The weather is often windy, gloomy with minimal sunlight, and humid. There are possibilities of thunderstorms during these months.

Tips: It is essential to carry an umbrella constantly throughout these months particularly at night as the intensity of the rains rises. Bring proper clothes since it is windy and humid at the same time.

2. Late March to May

These are often hot days with intermittent thunderstorms.

Temperature: Avg. of 32° high to 25° low

Weather: The weather is bright with low rainfall and a breeze. Nonetheless, more thunderstorms occur during these months.

Significance: The acclaimed Singapore Fashion Week is held during March-April, Dragon Boat Festival, Vesak Day, Singapore Arts Festival, Singapore International Film Festival, etc.

Why you should visit now: When the weather changes out of Northeast Monsoons, the weather is brighter and less overcast. One may enjoy the many intriguing festivals and activities conducted during this period. This is recognized as the ideal time to visit Singapore.

Know before you visit: Not much rainfall but the possibility of thunderstorms throughout these months.

Tips: It is suggested to have coats and an umbrella since the weather is unpredictable.

3. June to September

Sporadic showers and thunderstorms, often at midday, are a regular sight.

Temperature: Avg. of 32° high to 25° low.

Weather: The Southwest Monsoons commence in June and Singapore sees less rainfall and thunderstorms. It is often lovely in this season with plenty of sunlight.

Significance: Important events and festivals during these months include Hari Raya Aidilfitri, Singapore International Festival of Arts, National Day, The Hungry Ghost Festival, The Great Singapore Sale, Singapore Food Festival, Singapore Night Festival, Grand Prix Season, Lantern Festival, etc.

Why you should visit now: Due to the beautiful temperature, Singapore stages a range of intriguing and unique events throughout these months. Some of the most prominent and pleasant cuisine festivals are held by the nation.

Know before you visit: The weather is good with minimal rainfall and wind. Now is the greatest time to visit Singapore for those wishing to engage in culture, festivals, and activities.

Tips: Wear proper apparel since the weather is fairly sunny and bright.

4. October to November

Strong thunderstorms typically throughout lunchtime and early nights. This season is generally rainier as opposed to the intern-monsoon period at the beginning of the year.

Temperature: Avg. of 32° high to 25° low

Weather: The weather is moderately humid, less breezy, and has infrequent bouts of thunderstorms.

Significance: Important events and celebrations during these months include Deepavali, Hari Raya Haji, Singapore River Festival, etc.

Why you should visit now: Some of the most prominent religious holidays happen in October and November. One might get to observe the tradition and culture of Singapore during these months.

Know before you visit: The weather is nice with rare bouts of thunderstorms.

Tips: Wear adequate apparel since there are infrequent bouts of thunderstorms throughout these months.

2. How to get to Singapore

Singapore is a tiny island situated to the south of Johor State in southern Malaysia. While it is a tiny nation, there are several routes to enter the country that makes it quite simple for people to go in and out of Singapore. This is one of the key reasons why Singapore is considered a significant tourism center in the South East Asian area. You may enter by all modes of transportation, from plane, bus, rail, and sea.

Below is a full breakdown of the frequent entrance points to Singapore.

By Air

All international flights arriving in Singapore will arrive at Changi International Airport, which is located on the eastern tip of Singapore. The airport has 3 terminals that serve the major international airline companies, as well as a budget terminal that serves the low-cost airline carriers. The airport is modern, clean, and efficient, so entering here is quite straightforward.

By Bus

3 main bus terminals in Singapore connect to destinations all over Malaysia and even up to Thailand. The Queens Street Bus Terminal in the Bugis area in Singapore provides bus and taxi

services that head up to Johor Bahru (the neighboring city right across the border in Malaysia) only. As for buses that travel from other locations in Malaysia and even from Thailand, the Lavender Bus Terminal near the Lavender MRT area, and the Golden Mile Complex Bus Terminal are the main places that serve these destinations.

By Train

There is only one train station in Singapore that connects to Malaysia and beyond. This train station is located at the Woodlands Checkpoint on the northern tip of Singapore near Kranji MRT station.

By Sea

3 ferry terminals in Singapore provide ferry service from neighboring countries of Malaysia

and Indonesia. The Changi Village terminal provides ferry service by bumboat to and from Kampung Pengerang which is located in the Johor State of Malaysia. As for other destinations in Malaysia and Indonesia, then the ferry terminals at Harbourfront (central southern tip near Sentosa Island) and Tanah Merah (near the eastern side of Singapore) are the places that serve those destinations.

Going to Singapore provides several possibilities, as you may travel by air, land, and water. By understanding the typical entrance ways into Singapore, then you will be able to plan your trip successfully for both entering Singapore and your subsequent travel out of Singapore.

3. Best Time to Visit Singapore

While Singapore is a year-round destination, the ideal time to visit Singapore is from December to June. The months of February to April come under Singapore's dry season and is often when the nation experiences the least amount of rain, the lowest humidity, and the greatest sunlight.

Singapore offers generally regular weather and is hospitable enough for vacationers all year round for sightseeing. But, if you desire to avoid any crowds flooding the locations, the ideal time to visit Singapore is from July to November.

If you are merely seeking to visit Sentosa Island to sit back and relax, with a beach and outdoor activities just within sight then the summer days of June to August are the finest time to visit Singapore.

The Chinese New Year is one of the spectacular festivities of Singapore that occurs either in January or February. It depends on the first full moon of the year. Some significant events to attend include the mid-autumn festivities that take place in October, Hari Raja that falls in June, and Singapore's National Day in August.

If you are a shopaholic and want to visit Singapore simply for your love of shopping, then visit the nation from June to August. That's the greatest season to visit Singapore for shopping since The Great Singapore Sale is hosted during this time.

The length between July and August is not a particularly popular season to visit Singapore, thereby offering you a chance to snag some of the finest airfare and accommodation discounts. If you are a lone traveler, you need not worry about the ideal time to visit Singapore, since it has a lot in the store every month.

4. Things to do when you get to Singapore

The best way to discover Singapore is to do what the people do. That's correct, do activities that are 'non-touristy'. I have compiled a list of places and things to do in Singapore that is mostly free, other than a bottle of drink and transport fares. Hope you will find them helpful and have fun!

1. Take your 20-megapixel camera and walk down to Chinatown. Alright, fine, 2 million pixels is just as good. Take some pictures of the old shops and their almost 90-degree staircases. If you prefer capturing images of old folks, there are numerous lounges about the wet market doing nothing.

2. Go to Bukit Timah Nature Reserve for mountain riding or wander around and smell the green. Bring a bottle of water and sunglasses.

3. Take a ferry (cost about $2) to Pulau Ubin and tour the island. You may also hire a bike or a worn out motorbike. Try getting a cab if you can locate one, they can traverse tough terrains better than jeeps. Visit some of the Malay kampungs and prawn farms.

L4. Visit the Changi Prison. It's a free entrance for both tourists and inmates. Drop by the museum and chapel for some WW2 history and photos.

5. Visit the Siang Lim Si temple at Toa Payoh. Watch people get blessed. For the non-believers, you can count the number of deities inside ... it should occupy you for one hour.

6. Proceed to the East Coast Park for a swim and followed by satay-bee hoon at the hawker center.

7. Take a train to Changi Airport. Purchase two cups of coffee, locate a comfy seat in the departure hall viewing gallery, watch jets take off, and ask yourself why you are not on the plane traveling for a holiday.

8. Grab a map and go around MacRitchie Reservoir.

9. Go to Sim Lim Square and check out the newest computers and electronics.

10. Go jogging from Kallang River to Benjamin Sheares Bridge.

11. Catch a train from the Tanjong Pagar Train Station. You may travel across to Malaysia and return within a day.

12. Go water skiing in Punggol.

13. Build your kite and fly them in the Marine South open field. Following that, you may enjoy a fantastic steamboat meal at the various steamboat restaurants around.

14. Proceed to the Flea Market at Sungei Road. Some people nicknamed it the Thieves Market since most of the products sold there are not purchased by the merchants.

15. Go cycling in Sembawang Park. Peaceful and lovely even on the weekends. Cycle to the finish and you can see some of the huge ships fueling.

16. Bring your pit and grill beside the Upper Peirce Reservoir. But if you feel greasy, don't leap into the reservoir, you may end yourself at Point no. 4.

17. Visit the Tekka Market near Serangoon Road for a variety of fruits and vegetables. There is a stand offering one of the greatest Biryani Chicken Rice I have ever eaten.

18. Go fishing in Pasir Ris Park.

19. Visit the Kinokuniya Bookstore.

If you're dizzy after visiting the library-size bookshop, settle down for a cup of tea at the café within the bookstore. If you feel like a bookworm that day, then go for the Borders bookstore for a second helping.

20. Visit the Sungei Buloh Nature Park. Bring binoculars and conduct bird watching. Following that, you may purchase some hydroponic veggies from the surrounding farms.

5. Best Places to Stay in Singapore

Singapore provides different hotel options for all sorts of guests. These are 3 of the most popular districts to stay in Singapore.

Marina Bay and the Colonial District: The Marina Bay region and the Colonial District, which are situated near Raffles Place MRT and City Hall MRT, are one of the most popular destinations to discover high-priced hotels to stay at. This is attributable to the fact that this location is conveniently positioned in the city center of Singapore, as well as overlooking the coastline.

In this location, it is advantageously positioned among shopping, cafés, and historical landmarks. Prominent hotels in this region include the Marina Bay Sands Resort and Casino, the Fullerton Hotel near Raffles Place, the Ritz Carlton near Suntec City, and the Swiss Hotel near City Hall.

Sentosa Island: The recent installation of the Resorts World Resort and Casino on Sentosa Island has made it a popular place to stay. Sentosa Island offers numerous retreats from the bustling life of the city, such as luxurious outdoor spas, beaches near the water, and a golfing range.

In addition, within Resorts World proper, you will discover the Universal Studios theme park, and, of course the casino. Notable hotels in Sentosa include all the main hotels in Resorts World, such as the Hard Rock Café Hotel, and the beautiful Shangri-La Rasa Resort Hotel, situated near Siloso Beach on the corner of Sentosa Island.

Orchard Road: Finishing out the top 3 locations to stay in Singapore is the Orchard Road region. This region is notable for high-end luxury residences, as well as shopping. It is a shopper's utopia since there are various malls positioned along Orchard Road for all types of people equally. It is advantageously positioned since there are 3 distinct MRT subway stations across the course of the route. Popular places to stay in this area include the Grand Hyatt, the Hilton, the Marriott, and the Shangri-La.

By staying near these 3 most popular spots in Singapore, you will assure yourself to be in extreme proximity to all the areas of interest. These locations are situated in the city center and are extremely accessible from the MRT subway train stations.

Additionally, you will be quite close to several retail locations, and also cafés and pubs. Thus you will be near to all the activity and entertainment that Singapore has to offer, therefore you cannot go wrong if you stay in any of these 3 important districts.

Chapter 2: Travel Preparation

6. Entry Requirements

Singapore is a tiny nation in size but an economic superpower notably in South East Asia. Singapore is positioned near the south point of Malaysia, only one degree north of the equator.

The city is a combination of the culture and faiths of Malay, Chinese, Indian, and European. The four main religions are celebrated by the different ethnicity and the auspicious day like Muslims celebrating the end of Ramadan, Vesak day for the Buddhists, the festival of lights celebrated by Hindus, Christmas, and Easter for Christians, New Year's Day, and Lunar New

Year celebrated by the Chinese are officially a public holiday for all.

Food is a passion to many and a very much spoken about subject amongst the residents owing to the broad options of multi-ethnic food and European cuisines. Whilst it is pretty simple to travel in Singapore, it is always helpful to find out some essential travel information before you begin your trip. Here are some important travel suggestions for Singapore:

Visas for Singapore All passengers visiting Singapore are obliged to go through immigration clearance upon their entry into the nation. The issuing of social visit permits to tourists is regulated by Immigration & Checkpoints Authority (ICA) officials at the point of arrival. Visitors must pass the following basic entrance conditions before they are permitted to enter Singapore:

*A passport with at least 6 months of validity

*Valid Singapore visa, if applicable

*Adequate finances to endure for the desired time of stay in Singapore

*Confirmed onward/return tickets (if appropriate) (where applicable)

*Entrance facilities to their further destinations, e.g., visas.
Completed Disembarkation/Embarkation Card

*Yellow Fever Vaccination Certificate, if applicable

If you are deemed to be qualified for entrance into Singapore, you will obtain a Visit Permit, which will show the duration of your stay. You need to verify your Visit Pass and the number of days you may remain before leaving the checkpoint. Another Singapore visa restriction is that while you are in Singapore on a Visit Permit, you are not authorized to participate in any commercial, professional, or paid employment activities.

You also need to know that overstaying is a serious infraction in Singapore, so if you need to remain longer, you will have to request an extension. You may apply online for an extension via the e-Service, or you can attend to the Visitor Services Centre of the Immigration & Checkpoint Authority (ICA) before your Visit Pass expires

7. Types of Travelers Visa

Singapore provides a range of visas for people intending to travel to the nation. Depending on the purpose of the visit, the tourist may need to apply for a different form of visa. Here are some of the primary categories of visas accessible to visitors visiting Singapore:

1. Tourist Visa: This sort of visa is for people who intend to visit Singapore as a tourist. This visa permits passengers to remain in Singapore for up to 30 days, depending on their nationality. Visitors from certain countries may be given a visa upon arrival, while those from other nations may need to apply for a visa before visiting.

2. Business Visa: This visa is for persons going to Singapore for business-related activities such as attending meetings, conferences, trade fairs, and other events. Depending on the purpose and length of the stay, business travelers may be eligible to apply for a single-entry or multiple-entry visa.

3. Employment Pass (EP): This form of visa is for individuals who are traveling to Singapore to take up work. Candidates must satisfy specific conditions such as obtaining a job offer from a Singapore-based firm, having a minimum salary of SGD 3000, and having the relevant credentials and experience. The EP is normally good for two years.

4. Student Visa: This form of visa is for people going to Singapore to complete a full-time course of study at a registered educational institution. Applicants must meet certain requirements, such as having a valid admission letter from the educational institution and having the necessary funds to support themselves during the study. The student visa is normally valid for the length of the term of study.

5. Long-Term Visit Pass (LTVP): This form of visa is for persons who intend to remain in Singapore for a lengthy period, such as for family visits, medical treatment, or retirement. Candidates must satisfy specific conditions, such as having a sponsor or family member residing in Singapore and having the required finances to sustain themselves throughout the stay. The LTVP is normally valid for 1 to 5 years.

8. Singapore Visa on Arrival

Singapore is a popular location for visitors and business travelers alike. As such, many visitors to the nation are required to get a visa before their arrival. For people who need a visa, the Singapore government provides a visa-on-arrival (VOA) service.

The VOA service enables passengers to apply for a visa upon their arrival in the country. This service is offered to persons who match the qualifying conditions, including holding a valid passport from a foreign nation and having a valid return or onward ticket. Also, persons who desire to apply for the VOA must have adequate finances to support their stay in Singapore.

The VOA application procedure is quite basic. Upon arriving at Singapore's Changi Airport, tourists must complete the VOA application form and deliver it together with their passport, return or onward ticket, and evidence of adequate cash. The application will then be assessed by an immigration official and, if granted, the visa will be provided.

After the visa is obtained, passengers are permitted to remain in Singapore for up to 30 days. During this time, they are permitted to travel inside Singapore and take part in activities such as sightseeing, shopping, and business meetings. However, they are not allowed to work or study in Singapore.

The VOA service is a convenient way for travelers to visit Singapore without the hassle and expense of applying for a visa in advance. However, it is important to note that the VOA is only valid for a single entry and the visa must be used within 30 days of issue. After that period, travelers must apply for a new visa if they wish to stay in Singapore for longer.

9. Singapore Travel Restrictions

Singapore visa limitations play a vital role in managing the flow of persons entering and exiting the nation. To preserve the country's security, economy, and well-being, the Singapore government has adopted several visa laws and restrictions.

Singapore has a rigorous visa policy that requires most travelers to get a visa before entering the nation. Singapore visa requirements differ based on the individual's nationality and the purpose of the trip. Most travelers must get a visa before they arrive in Singapore.

The Singapore Immigration and Checkpoints Authority (ICA) is the government body responsible for granting visas and managing the flow of visitors into the nation. All tourists from countries that need a visa must get one from the ICA before going to Singapore. In addition, travelers must fulfill specific eligibility conditions to be granted a visa.

Visitors who are granted a visa must comply with the restrictions and length of the visa, which is normally valid for up to 90 days. Visas may be extended for particular reasons, such as jobs or studies. Visitors who do not comply with the requirements of their visa may be denied entrance or deported.

Singapore maintains severe limitations on who may enter the nation and for what reason. Visas are not provided to those who have criminal histories or have been previously deported from Singapore. In addition, visas are not provided to people who represent a danger to the security or public safety of the nation.

The Singapore government also limits the admission of people from specific nations, such as North Korea and Cuba. Visas are also not provided to those who have been declared bankrupt or to those who are thought to be in financial hardship.

Singapore visa limitations are in place to preserve the security and well-being of the nation and its residents. Visitors must comply with Singapore's visa requirements and restrictions to be given admission into the country.

Chapter 3: Transport and Accommodations

10. Getting Around

Public transit in Singapore is quick and clean, which makes moving about the city-state a snap. Singapore's transportation network enables access to every area of the island, either by bus, MRT underground, or cab.

A great suggestion for tourists is to avoid peak hour traffic between 8-9 am and 5-7 pm. Every time outside these hours remains a delight to stroll around in Singapore. Transitlink Guides are available at MRT stations, bus interchanges, and major bookshops. These useful manuals define every MRT and bus route in detail, so you won't get lost with one of these in hand for just SG$ 1.40.

City Shuttle

The City Shuttle operates every 20 minutes between 6 am and midnight. The 3 major routes serve all the important hotels in the Central Business Area, the colonial neighborhood, and Orchard Road. The pricing begins at SG$9 a trip for adults. You may also take the public bus no. 16 or 16E, which operates every 10 minutes or so and takes around half an hour to get to the city center. The fee begins at SG$1.50 for each ride.

Bus

Singapore's efficient and frequent bus service provides an entertaining way to explore the island's lovely neighborhoods. The primary service providers are SBS Transit and SMRT. Bus costs vary from $1 to $2.10. Make careful to place the correct change into the fare box.

MRT

The Mass Transit Railway (MRT) links to every section of the city and is the quickest and most cheap method to go about Singapore. Trains run from 5:30 am to midnight, with roughly 90 stops linking the city core and suburbs. Changi Airport is accessible by the MRT with frequent trains to the city. The travel takes a brief thirty minutes. A single ride may cost from $1 to $2.10 (with a $1 refundable deposit).

Taxis

Taxis are economical and widely accessible across Singapore, however, you may anticipate a wait during peak hours. They are easily hailed from outside hotels, and designated taxi stands or can be flagged down anywhere in the streets, and are a blessing when you are out till late at night. When in the city center you can only get a taxi from the designated ranks.

Trishaws

Explore Singapore on this traditional chauffeur-pedaled transport. Purely for tourist purposes, trishaws should be avoided for serious travel. With little room for bargaining, you can end up paying between $10-20 for short rides and about $50 for an hour's sightseeing.

EZ Link

If you are planning to stay in Singapore for longer than a week, you can save on train and bus travel by buying the EZ Link card. These cards can easily be bought from an MRT station and entitle you to a discount of up to 30%.

11. Accommodations in Singapore

Singapore is an amazing destination in Southeast Asia that offers a wide range of accommodations for travelers of all budgets and preferences. From luxurious resorts to budget-friendly hotels, there are many options available for visitors to choose from. Here are some of the most popular types of accommodations in Singapore.

Hotels:

Hotels are the most popular type of accommodation in Singapore and can be found in all parts of the city. Hotels range from budget-friendly to luxury options and offer a range of amenities such as swimming pools, spas, fitness centers, and in-room dining.

1. Marina Bay Sands: Located in the heart of Singapore, Marina Bay Sands is an iconic 5-star hotel featuring an infinity pool, SkyPark, and world-class shopping and dining. The hotel provides elegant rooms, with each room equipped with a flat-screen TV and minibar. Guests can also enjoy the on-site spa, fitness center, and business center. Furthermore, the hotel has a variety of restaurants and bars to choose from, as well as a casino and an art & science museum.

2. Shangri-La Hotel: The Shangri-La Hotel is a 5-star luxury hotel situated in the center of Singapore. The hotel features spacious rooms and suites with contemporary facilities such as free Wi-Fi, flat-screen televisions, and 24-hour room service. Visitors may also enjoy several on-site facilities, such as a spa, exercise center, and outdoor pool. Additionally, the hotel is home to various restaurants and bars, as well as a retail mall.

3. Four Seasons: Four Seasons is a 5-star luxury hotel situated in the heart of Singapore. The hotel provides elegant rooms, with each room offering a flat-screen TV, minibar, and free Wi-Fi. Visitors may also enjoy the on-site spa, exercise center, and outdoor pool. Additionally, the hotel is home to various restaurants and bars, as well as a business center.

4. Ritz Carlton: The Ritz Carlton is a 5-star luxury hotel situated in the heart of Singapore. The hotel provides elegant rooms, with each room offering a flat-screen TV, minibar, and free Wi-Fi. Visitors may also enjoy the on-site spa, exercise center, and outdoor pool. Additionally, the hotel is home to various restaurants and bars, as well as a business center.

5. InterContinental Singapore: InterContinental Singapore is a 5-star luxury hotel situated in the heart of Singapore. The hotel provides elegant rooms, with each room offering a flat-screen TV, minibar, and free Wi-Fi. Visitors may also enjoy the on-site spa, exercise center, and outdoor pool. Additionally, the hotel is home to various restaurants and bars, as well as a business center.

Hostels:

Hostels are a terrific alternative for visitors on a budget who don't mind sharing a room with other tourists. Hostels often include communal restrooms, kitchens, and common spaces, and some even provide individual rooms.

1. Beetel Teletech Hostel: Beetel Teletech Hostel is a modest yet decent hostel situated in the center of Singapore. The hostel provides basic services such as communal toilets and kitchenettes. Visitors may also enjoy the on-site restaurant and bar, as well as free Wi-Fi. Additionally, the hostel is positioned near public transit, making it convenient to explore the city.

2. Flashpackers Hostel: Flashpackers Hostel is a modest yet decent hostel situated in the center of Singapore. The hostel provides basic services such as communal toilets and kitchenettes. Visitors may also enjoy the on-site restaurant and bar, as well as free Wi-Fi. Additionally, the hostel is positioned near public transit, making it convenient to explore the city.

3. Beds & Dreams Hostel: Beds & Dreams Hostel is a simple yet decent hostel situated in the center of Singapore. The hostel provides basic services such as communal toilets and kitchenettes. Visitors may also enjoy the on-site restaurant and bar, as well as free Wi-Fi. Additionally, the hostel is positioned near public transit, making it convenient to explore the city.

4. Funky Flats Hostel: Funky Flats Hostel is a simple yet decent hostel situated in the center of Singapore. The homestay provides basic conveniences such as a kitchenette, living space, and private bathrooms. Visitors may also enjoy free Wi-Fi and the on-site restaurant and bar. Additionally, the homestay is positioned near public transit, making it convenient to explore the city.

Guesthouses:

Guesthouses are often cheaper than hotels and provide a more intimate and home-like feel. These apartments provide modest rooms with common bathrooms, and some may even include a shared kitchen.

1. Fragrance Hotel, Lavender: This modern budget hotel has nice rooms, an outdoor swimming pool, and a 24-hour lobby.

2. Hotel 81, Chinatown: This inexpensive hotel has air-conditioned rooms, complimentary Wi-Fi, and an on-site bar.

3. Hotel G, Chinatown: This trendy guesthouse offers large rooms, with a rooftop terrace that affords great city views.

4. Hotel 1929, Kampong Glam: This boutique guesthouse provides elegant accommodations, and free Wi-Fi, and is situated near the bustling Arab Street.

5. The Baxley, Chinatown: This luxurious guesthouse provides large rooms, a rooftop bar, and a 24-hour concierge service.

Resort:

Resorts are perfect for guests who want to be pampered and enjoy exquisite facilities like swimming pools, spas, and fitness centers. These properties usually offer on-site restaurants and bars, as well as activities like golf and tennis.

1. Resorts World Sentosa, Sentosa: This luxurious resort provides a variety of activities, including a casino, a Universal Studios theme park, and an aquarium.

2. Shangri-La's Rasa Sentosa Resort & Spa, Sentosa: This magnificent resort has several recreational amenities, including a spa, a swimming pool, and a fitness facility.

3. Marina Bay Sands, Marina Bay: This landmark resort provides a variety of attractions, including a casino, a retail complex, and a rooftop infinity pool.

4. The Sentosa, Sentosa: This tropical resort has big suites, a two-tiered swimming pool, and a range of leisure activities.

5. The Outpost Hotel, Sentosa: This contemporary resort has beautiful accommodations, a pool bar, and various restaurants.

Service Apartment

Serviced apartments are a terrific alternative for tourists who desire the solitude and comfort of an apartment, but don't want to bother with dishes or housekeeping. These apartments come with a choice of facilities, including swimming pools, gyms, and in-room dining.

1. The Ascott, Orchard: This beautiful serviced apartment provides large rooms, a fully-equipped kitchen, and a 24-hour concierge service.

2. St. Regis, Orchard: This elegant serviced apartment provides exceptional facilities, including a spa, a fitness center, and a private pool.

3. Orchard Rendezvous Hotel, Orchard: This serviced apartment provides nice accommodations, and free Wi-Fi, and is situated near the busy Orchard Road.

4. The Quincy Hotel, Orchard: This contemporary serviced apartment includes big rooms, a rooftop pool, and a range of eating options.

5. The Robertson Quay Hotel, Robertson Quay: This premium serviced apartment has big rooms, and a fitness facility, and is situated near the Singapore River.

Vacation rentals

Vacation rentals are a terrific alternative for vacationers who seek the solitude and convenience of a home away from home. These houses come in a range of sizes and types and provide facilities like private pools, hot tubs, and fully furnished kitchens.

1. The Venue Residences & Shoppes, Orchard: This magnificent vacation rental has a fully-equipped kitchen, and a balcony with city views, and is situated near the busy Orchard Road.

2. The Interlace, Buona Vista: This contemporary vacation rental includes big accommodations, and a swimming pool, and is situated near the Singapore Science Centre.

3. The Lofts @ Nathan, Orchard: This elegant holiday rental provides several facilities, including a fully-equipped kitchen, and a rooftop terrace, and is situated near the busy Orchard Road.

4. The Luxe, Orchard: This luxurious vacation rental has big rooms, and a fitness facility, and is positioned near the busy Orchard Road.

5. The Collection, Orchard: This boutique vacation rental has large accommodations, and a private pool, and is situated near the lively Orchard Road.

No matter what style of lodging you're searching for, Singapore provides something for everyone. From budget-friendly hotels to opulent resorts, Singapore is a terrific location for tourists of all budgets and inclinations.

Chapter 4: Learn About The Currency

12. Singapore currency

The Singapore dollar (SGD) is the official currency of Singapore, a city-state situated in Southeast Asia. It is also the national currency of Brunei, a neighboring country. The Singapore dollar was initially launched in 1967, replacing the Malaysian dollar. The currency is split into 100 cents and is abbreviated as S$ or SGD.

The Singapore dollar is maintained and issued by the Monetary Authority of Singapore (MAS) (MAS). The MAS is the central bank of Singapore and is responsible for the currency's stability and administration. It is also responsible for the issue and withdrawal of the currency. The Singapore dollar is likewise tied to a basket of international currencies and is permitted to gain or devalue as appropriate.

The Singapore dollar is a popular currency for international trade, especially in the area. The currency is also frequently utilized in the global commodities and financial sectors. It is accepted in many countries and is often used to settle payments in countries like the United States, Japan, China, and Australia.

The Singapore dollar is a strong and stable currency, backed by Singapore's strong economic fundamentals. The country's economy is one of the most open and competitive in the world, and its financial system is highly developed and sophisticated. The Singapore dollar is also a popular currency for international investors, as it offers a haven for their investments.

Since its introduction in 1967, the Singapore dollar has come a long way. It has become an important regional currency and is widely acknowledged in many nations. As Singapore's economy has continued to grow, the Singapore dollar has become an increasingly important currency in the global economy.

13. Where to Exchange Money in Singapore

Singapore is a melting pot of cultures, and its currency is the Singapore Dollar (SGD) (SGD). This makes it an attractive destination for travelers who want to exchange their foreign currency for local one.

There are several places in Singapore where you can exchange money. The most common and convenient place to exchange money is at a bank or money changer. Numerous banks in Singapore offer currency exchange services, including DBS Bank, OCBC Bank, UOB, Standard Chartered Bank, HSBC, and Citibank.

Money changers are also located in many shopping malls, such as Mustafa Centre, Lucky Plaza, and Chinatown. These money changers are typically open until late into the evening, making them a convenient option for those who need to exchange money after banking hours.

In addition, there are several online money exchange websites in Singapore. These websites allow users to compare the exchange rates offered by different banks and money changers before making a final decision. The most popular online money exchange websites in Singapore are XE Money Transfer, CurrencyFair, and TransferWise. These services enable users to compare the conversion rates for various currency pairings and make transactions fast and secure.

Lastly, there are various foreign currency booths situated in Singapore's main airports, including Changi Airport and Seletar Airport. These kiosks give passengers the ability to convert their money swiftly and easily. However, travelers should be aware that the exchange rates offered at these kiosks are usually not as competitive as those offered by banks and money changers.

Nevertheless, Singapore provides a broad selection of possibilities for people wishing to exchange their money. From online portals to banks and money changers, tourists may find a quick and cost-effective method to convert their money in Singapore.

14. Tipping

Tipping is not compulsory in Singapore, although it is traditional to offer a little tip for outstanding service. The amount you leave is totally up to you and in most circumstances, it is usual to leave between 5-10% of the overall price.

Most restaurants in Singapore do not add a service fee to the bill, therefore it is vital to verify before paying. If a service fee is already applied, then a tip is not expected.

Tipping is also not obligatory in taxis since a premium is already applied to your price. But, if your driver gives great service, it is courteous to round up the fee to the next dollar.

Tipping is not compulsory at hotels, although it is normal to offer a little tip for good service. This is frequently presented to the bell crew or cleaning personnel. You may leave a little amount of money or a symbol of gratitude such as a box of chocolates or an arrangement of flowers.

In Singapore, it is not essential to offer a gratuity for service employees in pubs and cafés. Nonetheless, you may leave a little tip for great service.

Generally, tipping is not obligatory in Singapore, although it is a great gesture to demonstrate thanks for outstanding service. The amount you choose to leave is up to you, but it is common to leave between 5-10% of the total bill.

15. Money and Budgeting

Spending money in Singapore may be a difficult undertaking, particularly for newcomers. Singapore is one of the most expensive cities in the world, and it is necessary to budget properly to ensure that your stay is fun and cheap.

The first stage in budgeting for a vacation to Singapore is to establish how much money you can comfortably spend. Assess your income, savings, and any other sources of money you may have. Finally, develop a budget that will enable you to enjoy your vacation without breaking the bank. Be sure to include required expenditures like transportation, housing, food, and entertainment, as well as any extras you may want to spend on, such as souvenirs or unique events.

After you have a budget in place, you can begin to plan your vacation. Start by investigating the various regions of Singapore and what they have to offer, including attractions, restaurants, and nightlife. This might help you select where you want to invest your time and money.

When it comes to transportation, Singapore offers a range of possibilities. The MRT (Mass Rapid Transport) is the most convenient and cheap method to go about the city. Nevertheless, cabs, buses, and auto rentals are also available. Be sure to factor in the cost of getting from one place to another when budgeting for your trip.

There are numerous accommodation options in Singapore depending on your budget. Luxury hotels are widely available, as are mid-range and budget hotels. Many visitors also choose to stay in hostels, which are a great way to meet other travelers and save money.

Singapore is known for its vibrant food scene, and there are plenty of cheap and delicious meals to be found. Hawker centers, food courts, and local eateries offer a variety of dishes at reasonable prices. There are also many fine dining restaurants if you are looking for a more upscale experience.

Finally, Singapore has a wide range of entertainment options, from festivals and concerts to shopping and nightlife. Consider the cost of any activities you plan to do and make sure they fit into your budget.

With careful planning and budgeting, a trip to Singapore can be an enjoyable and affordable experience. By researching the different areas of the city, researching transportation options, and choosing affordable accommodation, you can ensure that your trip is within your budget.

Additionally, by taking advantage of Singapore's cheap and delicious food and diverse entertainment options, you can make the most of your trip and get the most for your money.

16. Language

Singapore is a multilingual country with four official languages: English, Malay, Mandarin, and Tamil. The use of language in Singapore is an important part of its culture and reflects the diverse ethnic and cultural heritage of the country.

English is the lingua franca of Singapore and is widely spoken and understood by the majority of the people. It is the language used in government and industry and is the medium of teaching in all schools and institutions. Even though English is the most extensively spoken language, it is not the mother tongue of any of the ethnic groups in Singapore.

Mandarin is the second most frequently spoken language in Singapore and is the mother tongue of the Chinese people, who makes up the majority of the population in the nation. It is the official language in Singapore and is utilized in the media and daily life.

Malay is the national language of Singapore and is spoken by the Malay community, which accounts up 13.4% of the population. English is also an official language in Singapore and is utilized in the media and daily life.

Tamil is the language of the Tamil people, which makes up 4.2% of the population. It is the official language in Singapore and is utilized in the media and daily life.

In addition to the four official languages, there are several additional languages spoken in Singapore, including Japanese, Korean, Hindi, Tagalog, and several dialects of Chinese. These languages are spoken by minor populations in the nation and are not official languages.

Despite English being the language of choice in Singapore, the other languages are still very much alive and utilized in daily life. Singapore has a distinct culture, and language is a vital component of it.

17. General Travel Advice

Singapore is a lively, cosmopolitan city-state with a unique combination of cultures, cuisines, and architecture. It's also one of the safest and most structured nations in the world. As a consequence, it's a terrific place for people of all ages, from families to lone travelers.

Before you go to Singapore, it's necessary to educate yourself about the local laws and traditions. Here are some basic travel guidelines for travelers visiting Singapore:

1. **Dress modestly** — Singapore is a conservative nation, and many religious places require visitors to be covered up. It's ideal to wear loose clothes that cover your arms and legs, such as t-shirts and long skirts or trousers.

2. Respect local traditions - Singapore is made of many distinct cultures, and it's crucial to be respectful of them. For example, avoid touching anyone's head, and don't point at people with your finger.

3. Avoid public displays of affection – Singapore is a conservative country, and public displays of affection such as kissing or cuddling are not allowed.

4. Observe the laws – Singapore has strict laws and punishments, including the death penalty, for drug trafficking, vandalism, and public intoxication. Be sure to obey the laws and avoid any illegal activities.

5. Stay safe – Singapore has a low crime rate, but visitors should remain vigilant and take basic precautions such as carrying a copy of their passport, avoiding dark alleys, and not leaving their valuables unattended.

6. Keep hydrated — Singapore's hot, humid atmosphere may make it challenging to remain hydrated. Be sure you drink lots of water and avoid excessive alcohol intake.

7. Carry cash — Credit cards are accepted in most locations, but it's always a good idea to have some local money on hand. Singapore's currency is the Singapore Dollar (SGD) (SGD).

These are some of the most significant general travel recommendations for tourists visiting Singapore.

Chapter 5: Attraction and sightseeing

18. National Parks

1. Bukit Timah Nature Reserve: Bukit Timah Nature Reserve is Singapore's first and biggest nature reserve, encompassing an area of 164 hectares. It is home to a diversity of flora and wildlife, including uncommon kinds of plants, birds, reptiles, and animals. The reserve also has a network of pathways and boardwalks, enabling visitors to explore the park and appreciate the natural beauty of the region.

2. Sungei Buloh Wetland Reserve: Sungei Buloh Wetland Reserve is a protected region situated near the Straits of Johor, just outside of Singapore's municipal boundaries. The reserve encompasses an area of 87 hectares and is home to a variety of animals, including birds, reptiles, amphibians, mammals, and fish. The reserve also comprises diverse ecosystems, such as mangroves, mudflats, and coastal regions.

3. MacRitchie Reservoir Park: MacRitchie Reservoir Park is a natural reserve included inside the Central Catchment Nature Reserve. It covers an area of 256 hectares and is home to a variety of wildlife, including birds, reptiles, amphibians, mammals, and fish. The park also features a network of trails and boardwalks, allowing visitors to explore the park and enjoy the natural beauty of the area.

4. Labrador Nature Reserve: Labrador Nature Reserve is a protected area situated in the western section of Singapore. It spans an area of 24.4 hectares and is home to a variety of animals, including birds, reptiles, amphibians, mammals, and fish. The reserve also has a network of pathways and boardwalks, enabling visitors to explore the park and appreciate the natural beauty of the region.

5. Central Catchment Nature Reserve: Central Catchment Nature Reserve is a protected area located in the Central Region of Singapore. It covers an area of 2,015 hectares and is home to a variety of wildlife, including birds, reptiles, amphibians, mammals, and fish. The reserve also has a network of pathways and boardwalks, enabling visitors to explore the park and appreciate the natural beauty of the region.

19. Beaches

1. East Coast Park: East Coast Park is a beach park located on the southeastern coast of Singapore. Founded in 1976, the park encompasses an area of 185 hectares and provides a variety of leisure activities, including swimming, beach volleyball, and cycling. The park also contains a variety of restaurants, bars, and cafés, as well as a selection of entertainment venues.

2. Siloso Beach: Siloso Beach is a beach situated on the island of Sentosa in Singapore. Created in 1974, the beach encompasses an area of 1.2 hectares and includes a variety of leisure activities, including swimming, beach volleyball, and cycling. The beach also has a variety of restaurants, bars, and cafés, as well as a selection of entertainment venues.

3. Palawan Beach: Palawan Beach is a beach situated on the island of Sentosa in Singapore. Created in 1992, the beach encompasses an area of 1.8 hectares and includes a variety of leisure activities, including swimming, beach volleyball, and cycling. The beach also has a variety of restaurants, bars, and cafés, as well as a selection of entertainment venues.

4. Tanjong Beach: Tanjong Beach is a beach situated on the island of Sentosa in Singapore. Founded in 1962, the beach has an area of 1.4 hectares and includes a variety of leisure activities, including swimming, beach volleyball, and cycling. The beach also has a variety of restaurants, bars, and cafés, as well as a selection of entertainment venues.

5. Changi Beach: Changi Beach is a beach situated on the eastern coast of Singapore. Created in 1994, the beach encompasses an area of 12 hectares and includes a variety of leisure activities, including swimming, beach volleyball, and cycling. The beach also has a variety of restaurants, bars, and cafés, as well as a selection of entertainment venues.

20. Islands

1. Pulau Ubin: Pulau Ubin is an island situated in the northern part of Singapore. Created in 1972, the island encompasses an area of 2.2 hectares and is home to a variety of animals, including birds, reptiles, amphibians, mammals, and fish. The island also boasts a variety of pathways and boardwalks, enabling tourists to explore the island and appreciate the natural beauty of the region.

2. Lazarus Island: Lazarus Island is an island situated in the southeastern part of Singapore. Created in 1972, the island has an area of 0.5 hectares and is home to a variety of animals, including birds, reptiles, amphibians, mammals, and fish. The island also boasts a variety of pathways and boardwalks, enabling tourists to explore the island and appreciate the natural beauty of the region.

3. St. John's Island: Saint. John's Island is an island situated in the southwestern part of Singapore. Created in 1972, the island encompasses an area of 5.3 hectares and is home to a variety of animals, including birds, reptiles, amphibians, mammals, and fish. The island also boasts a variety of pathways and boardwalks, enabling tourists to explore the island and appreciate the natural beauty of the region.

4. Kusu Island: Kusu Island is an island situated in the southern part of Singapore. Created in 1972, the island encompasses an area of 0.3 hectares and is home to a variety of animals, including birds, reptiles, amphibians, mammals, and fish. The island also boasts a variety of pathways and boardwalks, enabling tourists to explore the island and appreciate the natural beauty of the region.

5. Sisters' Islands Marine Park: Sisters' Islands Marine Park is an island situated in the southwestern part of Singapore. Created in 2014, the island encompasses an area of 0.45 hectares and is home to a variety of fauna, including birds, reptiles, amphibians, mammals, and fish. The island also boasts a variety of pathways and boardwalks, enabling tourists to explore the island and appreciate the natural beauty of the region.

21. Temples

1. Sri Mariamman Temple: Sri Mariamman Temple is the oldest Hindu temple in Singapore, situated in the city's Chinatown neighborhood. Founded in 1827, the temple is devoted to the Hindu god Mariamman and boasts a mix of traditional architecture and sculptures. The temple also has a variety of shrines, as well as a range of cultural events and festivals.

2. Thian Hock Keng Temple: Thian Hock Keng city's Little India neighborhood. Founded in 1859, the temple is devoted to the Hindu deity Murugan and boasts a mix of traditional architecture and sculptures. The temple also has a variety of shrines, as well as a range of cultural events and festivals.

22. Museums

1. National Museum of Singapore: The National Museum of Singapore is the oldest in Singapore and is situated in the center of the city. Founded in 1887, the museum contains a mix of historical and cultural exhibitions, including objects from the country's past, artworks, and interactive displays. The museum also features several temporary exhibitions, as well as a library and research center.

2. Singapore Art Museum: The Singapore Art Museum is a museum located in the Central Region of Singapore. Established in 1996, the museum features a range of historical and cultural exhibits, including artifacts from the country's art and design history, artworks, and interactive displays. The museum also offers a variety of temporary exhibits, as well as a library and research center.

3. Singapore Philatelic Museum: The Singapore Philatelic Museum is a museum located in the Central Region of Singapore. Established in 1995, the museum features a range of historical and cultural exhibits, including artifacts from the country's stamp collection, artworks, and interactive displays. The museum also offers a variety of temporary exhibits, as well as a library and research center.

4. Peranakan Museum: The Peranakan Museum is a museum located in the Central Region of Singapore. Founded in 1997, the museum contains a mix of historical and cultural exhibits, including items from the country's Peranakan culture, artworks, and interactive displays. The museum also offers a variety of temporary exhibits, as well as a library and research center.

5. Asian Civilisations Museum: The Asian Civilisations Museum is a museum situated in the Central Area of Singapore. Founded in 1997, the museum contains a mix of historical and cultural exhibits, including objects from the region's history, artworks, and interactive displays. The museum also offers a variety of temporary exhibits, as well as a library and research center.

Chapter 6: Activities in Singapore

23. Outdoor Adventures

Singapore is a vibrant city with a plethora of outdoor activities to enjoy. From exciting water sports and recreational activities to lush green parks, there's something for everyone to enjoy.

Cycling:

Cycling is a great way to explore the city's green spaces and discover new sights. With bike paths connecting parks, gardens, and waterfronts, you can easily explore the city while getting a good workout. Cycling enthusiasts can also join guided tours, bike rentals, or cycling classes.

Hiking:

Hiking is another fantastic way to enjoy the outdoors and get nice exercise. Singapore features various hiking paths of varied difficulty levels, from basic trekking trails to more hard excursions. The paths are typically well-marked and provide spectacular views of the city and its rich nature.

Jogging:

Jogging is a popular hobby among residents and tourists alike. With jogging trails and parks all around the city, it's simple to locate a spot to jog. The most popular sites are East Coast Park, Gardens by the Sea, and Macritchie Waterfall.

Kayaking:

Kayaking is a terrific way to explore the city's waterways and get nice exercise. There are kayaking trips, lessons, and rentals available. Popular sites include the Kallang River, Marina Bay, and the Singapore River.

Stand-up Paddling:

Stand-up paddling is another popular outdoor sport in Singapore. It's a terrific way to appreciate the sights of the city's cityscape while getting decent exercise. Popular sites for stand-up paddling include Marina Bay and the Singapore River.

Rock Climbing:

For those looking for a more challenging outdoor activity, rock climbing is a great option. With multiple indoor and outdoor rock climbing gyms, as well as guided tours and workshops, it's simple to locate a location to climb.

Fishing:

Fishing is another popular outdoor sport in Singapore. There are various fishing areas throughout the city, such as the Kallang River, Punggol Waterway, and the Singapore River. You may also attend fishing expeditions and lessons.

Camping:

Camping is a terrific way to enjoy the outdoors and explore Singapore's natural reserves. There are various campsites throughout the city, such as the Singapore Botanic Gardens, Changi Beach Park, and Pulau Ubin.

Golf:

Golf is another popular outdoor sport in Singapore. There are various golf courses near the city, such as the Orchid Country Club and the Tanah Merah Country Club. You may also attend golf lessons and excursions.

Water Sports

Singapore is home to some of the world's best beaches, making it a great destination for water sports. From surfing and kayaking to snorkeling and parasailing, you can find plenty of activities to enjoy. If you're feeling daring, take your hand at kite-surfing or stand-up paddle boarding.

Nature Trails

Singapore is full of lush foliage, making it an excellent spot to explore nature. There are natural paths around the city, with lots of animals to observe along the route. Whether you choose to walk or cycle, you may discover lots of choices to meet your requirements.

These are just a handful of the various outdoor activities accessible in Singapore. There are plenty of other activities to enjoy, such as sailing, wakeboarding, and beach volleyball. Whether you're looking for an active adventure or a stroll, there's something for everyone to enjoy in Singapore.

24. Food and Drink

Singapore cuisine is the unique gastronomic culture of Singapore, a Southeast Asian city-state. The cuisine incorporates Chinese, Indian, Malay, and Indonesian cuisines and ingredients, producing a unique mixture of tastes.

Meals vary from basic street cuisines such as chicken rice and noodle soups to more complicated dishes such as rendang and nasi lemak. Singapore is frequently referred to as a 'food paradise' owing to its wonderful and diversified cuisine and culture.

Traditional Dishes:

1. Chicken Rice: This meal is regarded as one of the national foods of Singapore. It is made of poached or steamed chicken served with fragrant rice cooked in chicken stock with garlic and ginger.

2. Nasi Lemak: Nasi lemak is a popular Malaysian dish consisting of coconut-flavored rice cooked in coconut milk, accompanied by a spicy sambal sauce, cucumber slices, fried anchovies, roasted peanuts, and boiled eggs.

3. Rendang: Rendang is a spicy beef dish cooked in coconut milk and spices. It is one of the most popular dishes in Indonesia, Malaysia, and Singapore.

4. Laksa: Laksa is a spicy noodle soup made with rice noodles, chicken, prawns, or seafood, and a spicy coconut-based curry broth.

5. Char Kway Teow: Char kway teow is a famous meal in Singapore consisting of flat rice noodles stir-fried with egg, bean sprouts, prawns, and Chinese sausage.

6. Satay: Satay is a famous street snack in Singapore consisting of grilled skewers of meat or shellfish served with a spicy peanut sauce.

7. Bak Kut Teh: Bak kut teh is a pig rib soup prepared in a broth of herbs and spices such as star anise, cinnamon, cloves, and garlic.

Local Street Foods :

1. Hokkien Prawn Mee: Hokkien prawn mee is a famous street meal in Singapore consisting of noodles, prawns, and pork in a thick and savory broth.

2. Carrot Cake: Carrot cake is a famous street item in Singapore. It is comprised of grated carrots, eggs, and garlic stir-fried in a wok.

3. Hum Chim Peng: Hum chim peng is a deep-fried dough fritter loaded with sweet or savory ingredients.

4. Kaya Toast: Kaya toast is a popular snack in Singapore consisting of toasted bread covered with coconut and egg jam.

5. Mee Goreng: Mee goreng is a famous street cuisine in Singapore consisting of fried noodles with veggies, eggs, and seafood.

6. Roti Prata: Roti prata is a famous Indian-influenced street snack in Singapore. It is a thin, crisp flatbread eaten with curries.

7. Otah: Otah is a famous street meal in Singapore consisting of steamed or grilled fish paste blended with herbs and spices.

Drinks:

1. Teh Tarik: Teh tarik is a famous sweet milk tea in Singapore. The tea is poured between two containers frequently to aerate the milk, giving it a frothy texture.

2. Milo Dinosaur: Milo dinosaur is a popular drink in Singapore consisting of a blend of Milo powder, condensed milk, and sugar.

3. Bandung: Bandung is a famous rose-flavored drink in Singapore. It is created from rose syrup combined with milk and served cold.

4. Tiger Beer: Tiger beer is a popular drink in Singapore. It is a light-bodied beer with a malty taste.

5. Kopi: Kopi is a popular coffee in Singapore. It is a strong, sugary coffee made with sugar and condensed milk.

6. Soya Bean Milk: Soya bean milk is a popular drink in Singapore. It is a sweet and creamy milk manufactured from soya beans.

7. Yakult: Yakult is a popular probiotic drink in Singapore. It is a fermented milk drink with added sugar and living microbes.

25. Singapore Étiquettes.

Singapore is a tiny island off the coast of Malaysia and Indonesia. There are numerous distinct etiquettes, some unique and others different. Singapore is a unique nation that also has numerous restrictions.

*Singaporeans do not normally receive appetizers or any beverages.

*Singaporeans have their lunch laid on the table together with all other dishes containing food.

*After you have completed eating your food while you are with someone, it would be polite to demonstrate that you acknowledge their hospitality by leaving a portion of your meal on the plate.

*Different from other Asian cultures, in Singapore, it is not liked to tip after dinner, which seeks to impress other people nearby.

*While at a social supper, it is not nice to share your food with anybody.

*Singaporeans eat with chopsticks. They specifically use the thin end of the chopsticks though when getting food from the big dish that is available to everyone they use the thick side of the chopsticks.

*You should not tell a person any jokes until you know them very well because the jokes might be misunderstood.

*Do not bring up any ideas or start a conversation about subjects like religion or politics.

*No affection (kissing, hugging) between couples or anyone should be demonstrated in public areas.

*You should remain cool and not express rage in public settings.

*Singaporeans believe the head is sacred so it should not be touched, whether it is a child or an adult.

*To get someone to notice you and get his/her attention you should raise your hand.

*Singaporeans stand and talk to someone. Their hands should not be placed on their hips because it demonstrates the feeling of anger.

*You should not blow your nose and/or clear your throat in public areas.

*It is considered polite and appropriate to cover your mouth with your hand as you yawn.

Gift Giving:

1. People think the respectful thing to do is to refuse a gift a few times before accepting it to show that he/she is not greedy. After a couple of attempts of insisting that they take the gift, you should tell them how thankful you are that they did so.

2. To not look disrespectful or impatient, the person who is receiving the present should wait until the donor of the gift has departed. Then you may unwrap the present.

3. Some suggested presents are chocolates, a memory from your nation, a gift with your business emblem and maybe even a brand gift. No presents should be excessively costly.

4. Singapore is highly against bribery. This makes it not a possibility for anybody who works with the government to accept a gift.

5. When you provide a tiny individual present everyone should be thanked and treated to one.

6. Presents that are designed to surprise the person receiving the gift are not a smart idea to offer. It would cause an awkward reaction.

7. There should be a reason and an explanation for giving a gift to someone.

Business:

1. When asked a question you should not answer too rapidly for the reason that you might miss the correct answer. The correct thing to do is to refrain from answering for at least 15 seconds.

2. In business Singaporeans are not that assertive and sometimes when they "yes" to something they might be feeling differently than how they answered. In other words, "yes" doesn't always mean, "yes."

3. Singaporeans are strict on matters like money, or business due dates.

4. When offered praise it is normal to respectfully reject or deny it.

5. In business Singaporeans simply get right down to the primary notion of the meeting. They will make multiple selections extremely rapidly.

6. When assigned to appear at a business meeting a Singaporean should phone ahead of time if they are gonna be late. Being late without warning is unpleasant and inconsiderate.

7. Singaporeans expect individuals to give information, reports, etc. required when asked.

Greeting:

1. While shaking hands you should have a good solid grasp.

2. When at a social gathering or any function with numerous people, it is acceptable to shake hands with everyone present.

3. When shaking hands with someone, it is acceptable to offer a generous bow (Westerners may be a bit taller than Singaporeans therefore it is great to bow) (Westerners can be a little taller than Singaporeans so it is nice to bow.)

4. Offering a person your business card upon first meeting is an appropriate thing to do. You must have the writing on the card facing the individual and it should be presented with two hands.

5. When you meet you should introduce the persons of better rank or status and senior companions.

6. To be nice and respectful a Singaporean may not make direct eye contact with the person they

are meeting, but instead glance down. They do this to honor those of an older age or greater position.

7. Instead of greeting with the customary "How are you" or "Good Morning" Singaporeans will frequently welcome by asking " Where are you going" or " Have you eaten."

8. Greetings shouldn't be spoken using your nickname unless you are desired to in a unique scenario or you know the individual well and have built a bond.

Everyday Living:

1. You shouldn't tell a person any jokes until you know them well since the jokes can be misconstrued or simply preferred.

2. Don't bring up any thoughts or start a debate regarding matters like religion or politics.

3. No affection (kissing, embracing) between couples or anybody should be displayed in public. You should stay cool and not display rage in public locations.

When crossing your legs it is good to put one knee over the other.

26. Shopping in Singapore

Shopping Mall:

1. VivoCity: VivoCity is Singapore's biggest retail complex, situated in the HarbourFront sector. It features over 300 retail outlets and lots of cafes, making it the ideal destination for travelers to browse for souvenirs, handicrafts, and other products. This mall also boasts a rooftop playground, movie theater, and a big outdoor amphitheater, making it a perfect venue for family-friendly activities.

2. Marina Square: Situated in the center of Marina Bay, this retail mall offers something for everyone, including local craftsmen and merchants offering traditional crafts and souvenirs. The mall is also home to a range of foreign companies, making it a fantastic spot to buy souvenirs.

3. Suntec City: Suntec City is one of Singapore's major shopping malls, and is home to hundreds of stores and eateries. It is also one of the most popular tourist sites in Singapore and contains a broad assortment of souvenirs, handicrafts, and other things.

4. Orchard Road: Orchard Road is one of the most prominent shopping locations in Singapore, and is home to many of the city's high-end retail malls. Visitors may also discover a broad assortment of souvenirs, handicrafts, and other products here.

5. Mustafa Centre: Situated in the heart of Little India, Mustafa Centre is a 24-hour retail mall that is popular with visitors. Here, you can discover a broad assortment of souvenirs, handicrafts, spices, and other products.

27. Souvenirs:

1. Peranakan Dolls: Peranakan dolls are one of the most popular gifts among travelers visiting

Singapore. The dolls, which depict the traditional Peranakan dress and culture, are handmade and come in a variety of styles and sizes.

2. Merlion Souvenirs: The Merlion is one of the most iconic symbols of Singapore, and tourists can purchase a wide range of Merlion-themed souvenirs such as keychains, cups, mugs, and other items.

3. Food Souvenirs: Singapore is known for its delicious food, and tourists can purchase a variety of food-related souvenirs such as local snacks, jams, sauces, and other items.

4. Crafts: Singapore is home to a vibrant craft culture, and tourists can purchase a variety of handmade crafts such as jewelry, bags, pottery, and other items.

5. Vintage Postcards: Vintage postcards are a popular souvenir among tourists to Singapore, and are available from various antique shops, street vendors, and other outlets.

28. Handicrafts in Singapore

1. Batik: Batik is a traditional dyeing technique used to create vibrant patterns and designs. Tourists can purchase a variety of handmade batik items such as scarves, bags, and clothing from various markets and stores in Singapore.

2. Kebaya: Kebaya is a traditional form of clothing that is popular among visitors to

Singapore. Tourists can purchase a variety of handmade kebaya items such as dresses, blouses, and other garments.

3. Kite Making: Kite making is a popular handicraft among visitors to Singapore, and tourists can purchase a variety of handmade kites from various stores and markets.

4. Wood Carvings: Wood carving is a traditional handicraft in Singapore, and tourists can purchase a variety of wooden items such as masks, figurines, and other items.

5. Woven Baskets: Woven baskets are a popular handicraft among visitors to Singapore, and tourists can purchase a variety of handmade baskets from various stores and markets.

Chapter 7: Cultural Experience

29. Festival

Singapore is a vibrant and cosmopolitan city that is known for its festivals and holidays. From the bustling Chinese New Year celebrations to the amazing Christmas festivities, Singapore has something to offer everyone. Here's a look at some of the best festivals and holidays in Singapore.

Chinese New Year: One of the most popular festivals in Singapore, the Chinese New Year is celebrated by the Chinese community with great enthusiasm and joy. The festival is celebrated for 15 days and marks the beginning of the Lunar New Year. The celebrations include traditional lion and dragon dances and the exchange of gifts.

Thaipusam: Thaipusam is an important Hindu holiday that is held in honor of Lord Murugan. On this day, worshippers hold kavadis (special constructions) and proceed in a procession to the Sri Srinivasa Perumal Temple in Little India.

Deepavali: Deepavali, or the festival of lights, is celebrated by Hindus in Singapore. On this day, oil lamps are lit, special prayers are made to the gods, and sweets and savories are shared.

Christmas: Singapore celebrates Christmas with considerable zest and zeal. Streets are decked with festive lights, while shopping malls and department shops put up decorations and offer discounts. The holiday season is also highlighted by caroling and Christmas parties.

Hari Raya Puasa: Hari Raya Puasa commemorates the conclusion of the fasting month of Ramadan and is celebrated by Muslims with tremendous passion. On this day, people exchange presents, attend prayer meetings and engage in feasts.

Singapore Food Festival: The Singapore Food Festival is a celebration of the country's unique culinary traditions. The festival displays a variety of gastronomic pleasures from all around the globe, and visitors may experience a choice of local cuisine.

Singapore Grand Prix: The Singapore Grand Prix is a street race that is conducted at the

Marina Bay Street Circuit. The event is a big attraction for people from all over the globe who travel to the city to see the race and enjoy the festivities.

Singapore River Festival: The Singapore River Festival is a carnival of lights and music that is hosted on the banks of the Singapore River. This festival is a celebration of the city's rich cultural past and involves a variety of events such as music performances, art installations, and food vendors.

30. Music and dance

Singapore has a strong and diversified music and dance culture. From traditional music and dance to new, experimental genres, there is something for everyone.

Traditional Music and Dance: Traditional music and dance in Singapore represent the country's rich cultural legacy. Traditional music genres include the percussion forms of Peranakan, Hokkien, Teochew, and Cantonese music. Traditional dances include the Malay Zapin, Chinese Lion and Dragon dances, Indian Bharatanatyam, and the Malay Joget.

Pop Music: Pop music has been popular in Singapore, with numerous local and international performers making their mark. Pop music generally contains aspects of traditional music and dancing, as well as electronic and hip-hop sounds. Popular vocalists include Stefanie Sun, JJ Lin, and Kit Chan.

Experimental Music and Dance: Experimental music and dance are getting increasingly popular in Singapore. These encompass genres such as electronica, glitch, and ambient music. Dancing styles include modern, breakdancing, popping, and locking. Some of the most prominent musicians in this genre are Electrico, dné, and Sun Li.

Folk Music: Folk music has been around for generations in Singapore. It is popular among the older generations and is often accompanied by traditional dances. Popular instruments used in folk music include the gong, drums, and erhu.

Global Music: World music has grown more popular in Singapore, with many local and international performers playing. Genres include Latin, reggae, jazz, Calypso, and African.

Prominent performers include The Sam Willows, Lady Kash and Krissy, and Joi Chua.

Contemporary Music and Dance: Contemporary music and dance are popular in Singapore, integrating aspects of traditional and contemporary music and dance. Genres include hip-hop, rap, rock, and R&B. Prominent musicians include TheLionCityBoy, Shigga Shay, and Gentle Bones.

No matter what style of music and dance you're interested in, Singapore offers something for everyone. Whether you're seeking traditional music and dance, experimental music and dance, or contemporary music and dance, you can find it in Singapore.

Chapter 8: The Best 7 days Singapore's Itinerary

31. Best 7 days Itinerary

Day 1: Merlion statue

• Start the day by seeing the famed Merlion Statue at Marina Bay.

• Take a walk along the waterfront promenade at Marina Bay and take in the spectacular views of the city skyline.

• Spend the remainder of the morning touring the Marina Bay Sands, which comprises a retail mall, a casino, an observation deck, and an art museum.

- Pause for lunch at one of the numerous cafes available inside the Marina Bay Sands complex.
- Enjoy a leisurely afternoon walk through the Singapore Botanic Gardens, one of Singapore's most famous UNESCO World Heritage Sites.

- Spend the early evening in Clarke Quay, a busy waterfront area with a selection of restaurants, pubs, and nightclubs to pick from.

Day 2: Colonial District

- Take a tour of the Colonial District, where you can explore the remnants of Singapore's British colonial past.

- Visit the Buddha Tooth Relic Temple and Museum, a bustling Chinese temple in the center of the city.

• Spend the day touring Chinatown, where you may visit traditional Chinese temples, souvenir stores, and local cafes.

• Pause for lunch at a local hawker center, where you may try a range of native foods.

• Spend the evening at the Night Safari, where you may discover the nocturnal creatures of the jungle.

Day 3: Jurong Bird park

• Visit Jurong Bird Park, home to a range of unique birds from across the globe.

• Take a trip on the Singapore Flyer, the world's biggest observation wheel.

• Spend the afternoon touring the Singapore Zoo, where you can watch a variety of animals in their natural habitats.

• Pause for lunch at the Singapore Zoo's Food Safari restaurant.

• Spend the evening at Gardens by the Bay, where you can explore the Supertree Grove, the Cloud Forest, and the Flower Dome.

Day 4: Science Centre

• Visit the Singapore Science Centre, where you can discover the world of science via interactive displays and activities.

- Take a boat journey to the adjacent Pulau Ubin, where you can enjoy the rustic charm of Singapore's "last kampong".

- Spend the afternoon at Sentosa Island, where you can visit the Universal Studios theme park and explore the beaches and attractions.

- Stop for lunch at one of the many eateries located on the island.

- Spend the evening at Orchard Road, Singapore's premier shopping district.

Day 5: National Museum

- Visit the National Museum of Singapore, which houses a variety of exhibits and artifacts from Singapore's past.

• Take a guided tour of the National Gallery Singapore, which houses the world's largest collection of Singaporean art.

• Spend the afternoon at Little India, where you can explore the vibrant culture and cuisine of Singapore's Indian community.

• Stop for lunch at one of the many eateries located in the area.

• Spend the evening exploring the shops and eateries on Arab Street.

Day 6: Singapore Flyer

• Visit the Singapore Flyer, the world's largest observation wheel.

• Take a guided tour of the Raffles Hotel, one of Singapore's most iconic landmarks.

• Spend the afternoon exploring the botanical gardens of Singapore, where you can view a variety of tropical plants and flowers.

• Stop for lunch at one of the many eateries located in the area.

• Spend the evening at the Singapore Night Safari, where you can explore the nocturnal wildlife of the rainforest.

Day 7: Botanic Garden

• Visit the Singapore Botanic Gardens, a UNESCO World Heritage Site.

- Take a guided tour of Suntec City, a modern shopping and entertainment complex.

- Spend the afternoon exploring the shopping malls of Orchard Road.

- Stop for lunch at one of the many eateries located in the area.

- Spend the evening at the Esplanade, where you can catch a performance at one of the theatres or enjoy a meal at one of the eateries.

Chapter 9: Safety And Security

32. Rules and Regulations

Singapore has its own set of rules and regulations, which heavily criminalizes many actions which are considered petty crimes or no-offense acts in most other countries.

The general crimes of Singapore are:

Jaywalking - Walking or crossing the street illegally, that is not utilizing the zebra crossing, not obeying the traffic signals when crossing, or not using the pedestrian walkway.

Smoking in public places and locations where 'No Smoking' signs are put up for limitation.

Urinating or spitting in public.

Littering on the highways instead of utilizing the garbage.

Committing affray or a fight between two or more persons in a public location, such as bar brawls or street commotions.

33. Singapore Safety

Singapore is generally regarded for its safe and secure atmosphere. The Singapore Police Force is very efficient and works in concert with the immigration authorities to ensure that the nation stays safe and secure.

To safeguard the safety of its inhabitants, Singapore has taken a variety of security procedures. They include:

1. The installation of CCTV cameras in public locations. This allows the police to monitor suspicious activity in real-time.

2. The deployment of uniformed police officers and plain-clothes cops in strategic places. This helps them to react promptly to any security problems.

3. The introduction of a stringent immigration regime. This helps to prevent the arrival of illegal immigrants, as well as persons with criminal backgrounds.

4. The creation of a countrywide licensing system for guns. This helps to minimize the number of guns on the streets and also makes it simpler for the police to trace the owners of such weapons.

5. The development of a national database of forbidden chemicals. This helps to curb the sale and distribution of illicit narcotics.

6. The creation of a countrywide database of stolen and recovered objects. This helps to prevent the selling of stolen items.

7. The execution of rigorous rules protecting public safety. This helps to guarantee that individuals may feel secure while they are out and about.

34. Singapore Emergency Numbers

In addition to these security procedures, Singapore also provides a variety of emergency contact lines that tourists may call in case they suffer any issues while in the country. They include:

1. The Singapore Police Force – Dial 999 (or +65 999 from outside Singapore)

2. The Singapore Civil Defence Force – Dial 995 (or +65 995 from outside Singapore)

3. The Singapore Immigration and Checkpoints Authority – Dial 6391 6100 (or +65 6391 6100 from outside Singapore)

4. The Singapore Emergency Medical Services – Dial 995 (or +65 995 from outside Singapore)

5. The Singapore Fire Brigade - Call 995 (or +65 995 from outside Singapore)

It is important to remember that these emergency contact numbers should only be used in the event of an emergency or serious crime. All other complaints and inquiries should be directed to the relevant authorities.

Chapter 10: Conclusion

Singapore is a vibrant, diverse, and unique country that should be on every traveler's list of must-visit destinations. From its bustling city center to its stunning natural surroundings, it offers something to everyone. Its endless array of attractions, activities and cultural experiences will keep you busy for days, and its world-class dining and shopping options will make it hard to leave. Whether you're looking for a luxurious city getaway, an outdoor adventure, or a place to relax and unwind, Singapore has something for everyone.

The country's history and architecture are intriguing, and the cuisine is just delicious. The people are kind, and the infrastructure is well-developed. From its multicultural heritage to its modern amenities, Singapore is a place full of surprises and excitement. With its unique blend of East and West, it has something to offer to everyone who visits.

Singapore is a must-visit destination, and anyone who has the chance to explore it is sure to have a wonderful experience. From its culture and cuisine to its attractions and activities, there is something for everyone in this unique destination. Whether you are a first-time visitor or a seasoned traveler, you're sure to find something to love in Singapore.

Printed in Great Britain
by Amazon

Printed in Great Britain
by Amazon